GCSE OCR Computer Science Exam Revision Workbook

Russell I F Bryant

GCSE OCR Computer Science – Exam Revision Workbook

Python and the Python Logo are trademarks or
registered trademarks of the Python Software Foundation.

Cover designed by Russell I F Bryant

Visit our website at www.edulito.com
ISBN: 9781797726052

Contents

1. Below is a diagram to show some of the features of a CPU. A CPU can be found inside computer devices.

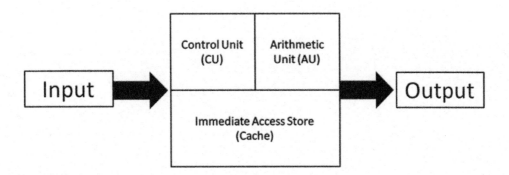

Central Processing Unit (CPU)

(a) Describe the role played by the CPU in a computer device [2]

....

....

....

What is the role played by each of the following components within the CPU?

(b) Control Unit [1]

....

....

....

(c) Arithmetic Unit [2]

....

....

....

....

(d) Cache [2]

....

....

....

....

(e) Some CPUs perform better than other CPUs. Apart from the amount of cache in a CPU, list two other factors that influence the performance of a CPU and for each explain how the characteristic listed can improve performance. [4]

Factor.1 ....

Explanation

....

....

....

Factor.2 ....

Explanation

....

....

....

2. The diagram below shows a pictorial representation of Von Neumann architecture.

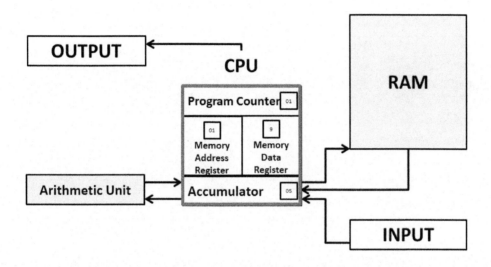

In relation Von Neumann architecture what is the role played by the:

(a) The Memory Address Register (MAR)? [2]

....

....

....

(b) The Memory Data Register (MDR)? [2]

....

....

(c) The Program Counter (PC)? [3]

....

....

....

....

(d) The Accumulator? [2]

....

....

....

3. Many devices that we find around us, both at home and in the wider world, can be described as embedded systems.

(a) Give an example of an embedded system. [1]

....

(b) Explain the purpose of this embedded system, including a description of three hardware components that are part of the embedded system. [3]

....

....

....

(c) Give another example of an embedded system. [1]

....

 (d) Explain the purpose of this embedded system, including a description of three components

that are part of the embedded system. [3]

....

....

....

Russell I F Bryant

1.2 Memory

1. This table compares ROM and RAM. Complete the table. [9]

	RAM	ROM
What does it stand for?	a.	b.
Definition	RAM is the main place for storing instructions and data whilst a program is being executed. It is sometimes called main memory. Program data is copied into RAM before the CPU can run the program.	c.
Use	d.	e.
Volatility	f.	g.

2. (a) Explain the purpose of the ROM CHIP inside a desktop computer. [2]

....

....

....

....

....

....

(b) Name two other devices that contain ROM chips. [2]

....

....

3. Explain the role played by RAM inside a desktop computer. [2]

....

....

....

....

....

(b) Name two other devices that contain RAM. [2]

....

....

4. (a) Explain what is meant by Virtual Memory and why it is used. [3]

....

....

....

....

....

....

(b) Describe ONE disadvantage of using Virtual Memory. [2]

....

....

....

5. (a) What is Flash Memory? [2]

....

....

....

(b) Name three devices that use Flash Memory. [2]

....

....

....

(c) Why do you think these devices use Flash Memory rather than a Hard Disk Drive? [2]

....

....

....

(d) Why are Hard Disk Drives, rather than Solid State Drives (Flash Memory), still commonly

used as the main storage device by desktop PCs and Servers? [2]

....

....

....

....

....

....

1.3 Storage

1. (a) Define the term "secondary storage". [2]

....

....

....

....

(b) Give two examples of secondary storage devices. [2]

....

....

(c)Why does a computer need a secondary storage device? [2]

....

....

....

....

2. (a) The table below has been produced to show the data capacity of a range of storage devices? For each device include an appropriate data capacity. The first one has been done for you. [4]

Device	Data Capacity
Hard Disk Drive	1.0 TB
DVD Drive	
Solid State Drive	

USB Memory Stick	
BluRay Drive	

(b) Aisha has been to a party and has taken 145 photos. Each photo is approximately 2560 KB.

She has also taken 15 movie clips. Each movie clip is 650 MB.

She has decided to store these photos and movies on a USB Memory stick. What capacity does she require to store all of the photos? Show your workings. [3]

....

....

....

3. Explain the advantages and disadvantages of using each storage device type. [6]

Storage Method	Example	Advantages	Disadvantages
Optical Drive	CD, DVD and BluRay drive.		
Magnetic	HDD Drive used in PCs and servers External HDD		

Solid State Drive	USB Memory Stick Flash Drives used in smart phones and tablets		

4. Read the information below. For each person choose the most suitable storage device and explain why.

(a) Joe D'Angelo is a musician and has just recorded some new songs with his band. His Internet access is down and he wants to send out the five tracks that he has recorded to 34 different record labels. He wants to spend as little money as possible.

What is the most suitable storage device? [1]

....

Why? [2]

....

....

....

(b) Aleyna travels all over the UK providing IT security support for large and medium sized companies. She is about to buy a new laptop to take to these meetings. She wants a laptop that is lightweight and portable.

What is the most suitable storage device? [1]

....

Why? [2]

....

....

....

....

(c) Priya is a real film buff and wants to buy a new PC that she can use to store her collection of films. She wants a drive in her PC with a large storage capacity so that she can quickly access and watch any film.

What is the most suitable storage device? [1]

....

Why? [2]

....

....

....

....

....

1.4 Wired and wireless networks

1. (a) What is a local area network (LAN)? [2]

....

....

....

....

(b) Give an example of one type of organisation that might use a LAN. [1]

....

2.(a) What is a wide area network (WAN)? [2]

....

....

....

....

(b) Give an example of one type of organisation that would use a WAN. [1]

....

3. (a) What is meant by latency? [2]

....

....

....

(b) Using an example explain what is meant by low latency in a network? [3]

....

....

....

....

4. What is meant by bandwidth? [2]

....

....

....

....

5. (a) What is data packet loss? [1]

....

....

....

....

(b) What causes data packet loss? [1]

....

....

....

(c) What does the network do to overcome the loss of data packets? [1]

....

....

....

....

6. (a) Draw a diagram below to show the main features of a client server network that has

three desktop PCs and a network printer. [3]

(b)List **TWO** advantages and **TWO** disadvantages of a client server network. [4]

Advantages	Disadvantages

7(a) Draw a diagram below to show the main features of a peer to peer network that has two desktop PCs and a wireless laptop connection. [3]

(b) List **TWO** advantages and **TWO** disadvantages of a peer to peer network. [4]

Advantages	Disadvantages

8. Each of the items below plays a role in the correct function of a local area network.

Match the item to its function (Draw a line to link them). [3]

Item		Function
Wireless access points		This is installed inside a computer so that it can be connected to a network.
Routers		This is a hardware device that allows wireless devices to connect to a wired network using Wi-Fi.
Switches		This is the method or materials used to transmit data in a network e.g. using Ethernet cables, optical cables or wireless.
NIC (Network Interface Controller/Card)		A device that forwards data packets along networks.
Transmission media		A device that connects devices together on a computer network, by using packet switching to receive, process and forward data to the destination device.

9. (a) What is a domain name server? [2]

....

....

....

....

(b) Why is a domain name server necessary? [1]

....

....

(c) What is a host computer? [1]

....

....

....

(d) What is meant by cloud computing? [2]

....

....

....

10. (a) What is a VPN? [2]

....

....

....

(b) Explain why a company may encourage its staff to use a VPN? [1]

....

....

....

1.5 Network topologies, protocols and layers

1. (a) What is meant by network topology? [2]

....

....

....

b) Two common types of network topology are star and mesh networks. Draw a diagram to

show the structure of each type of network. [2]

Star Network	Mesh Network

(c) Outline the advantages and disadvantages of each type of network in the table below. [4]

Type of Network Topology	Description	Advantages	Disadvantages
Star	Nodes linked to a central device hub/switch Used for LANs		
Mesh	Every node links to every other node Commonly used for WANs		

2. (a) What is meant by Wi-Fi frequency? Use the words to fill the gaps in the text. [5]

frequency   shorter   wireless   higher   radio

Wi-Fi is a technology that uses ……………………………………. waves to provide network connectivity.

Wi-Fi provides …………………………… connectivity to your devices by emitting a …………………………

between 2.4 and 5GHz.

In radio waves the ………………………………… the frequency the ………………………………… the range.

(b) Wi-Fi operates on different channels. You can choose the channel so that you get a better connection. Every Wi-Fi network transmits and receives data on a certain frequency, or channel. As Wi-Fi data is digital, many different devices can communicate successfully on the same channel. Complete this table that compares two frequency bands. [6]

Band	2.4 GHz	5 GHz
Channel	Three non-overlapping channels	23 non-overlapping channels
Standard	Wireless-B, G, and N	Wireless-A, N, and AC
Network Range		
Interference		
Recommended for home network?		

(c) What is Wi-Fi encryption? [2]

....

....

....

(d) Why is Wi-Fi encrypted? [1]

....

....

....

3. What is a wired ethernet network? [1]

....

....

....

4. (a) Explain the meaning of network protocol? [2]

....

....

....

(b) Complete the first column of this table to show the names of each network protocol.

Protocol Type	Function	Description
1	This is the basic communication language or protocol of the Internet.	Two Layers: Higher Layer -Transmission Control Protocol, manages the assembling of a message or file into smaller packets that are transmitted over the Internet and received by a TCP layer that reassembles the packets into the original message. The lower layer - Internet Protocol, handles the address part of each packet so that it gets to the right destination. Each gateway computer on the network checks this address to see where to forward the message.
2	This is the underlying protocol used by the World Wide Web.	It defines how messages are formatted and transmitted, and what actions Web servers and browsers should take in response to various commands.
3	This is the use of a Secure Socket Layer (SSL) as a sub-layer under regular HTTP application layering.	It encrypts and decrypts user page requests as well as the pages that are returned by the Web server.
4	This is a standard network protocol used to transfer computer files between a client and a server on a computer network.	It is built on a client-server model architecture and uses separate control and data connections between the client and the server.
5	This is a type of computer networking and Internet standard protocol that extracts and retrieves email from a remote mail server for access by the host machine.	It simply downloads email to your computer, and usually (but not always) deletes the email from the remote server.

6	This is an Internet standard protocol used by e-mail clients to retrieve e-mail messages from a mail server over a TCP/IP connection.	This allows users to store their email on remote servers. This two-way protocol also allows the user to synchronize their email among multiple devices, which is extremely important today, when most people have at least two devices - their laptop and smartphone.
7	This is an Internet standard for electronic mail (email) transmission.	

5. What is meant by Packet switching? [3]

....

....

....

....

....

1.6 System security

1. (a) What is meant by malware? [1]

....

....

....

(b) Give 3 examples of types of malware and explain how each can be harmful. [6]

Example 1..

How is this malware harmful?

....

....

....

Example 2..

How is this malware harmful?

....

....

....

Example 3..

How is this malware harmful?

....

....

....

2. The email below is an example of a phishing attack.

Tax Refund Notification

After the last annual calculations of your fiscal activity, we have determined that you
are eligible to receive a tax refund of **468.50 GBP.** Please submit the tax refund
request and click here by having your tax refund send to your bank account in due time

Please Click Here to have your tax refund to your bank account, your tax refund will be
sent
to your bank account in due time take your time to go through the bank we have on our list
Note : A refund can be delayed a variety of reasons, for example submitting invalid
records or applying after deadline.

Best Regards

HM Revenue & Customs

q7nbj2fqh6gncq60efwfh2qhztqcvc

Directgov © Crown Copyright | Terms & Conditions | Privacy Policy | Accessibility Business Link O

List three reasons why it is believed that this is a Phishing attack. [3]

Reason 1

....

....

Reason 2

....

....

Reason 3

....

....

3. (a) Hackers sometimes use social engineering to gain access to network data. What is meant by social engineering? [1]

....

....

(b) Explain how a person would go about carrying out a social engineering attack on a company. [1]

....

....

....

....

(c) What is a brute force attack? [2]

....

....

....

....

(d) What is a denial of service attack and why is it carried out? [2]

....

....

....

....

(e) What is a data interception and theft attack? [2]

....

....

....

....

(f) What is an SQL injection attack? [2]

....

....

....

....

4. (a) Businesses and other organisations usually have an Acceptable Use Policy (AUP). What is an AUP and why do businesses and other organisations feel that it is important to have one? [2]

....

....

....

....

(b) Businesses and other organisations use a variety of techniques to protect their network.

Complete the table by including a description of each technique. [8]

Technique	Description
Penetration testing	
Network forensics	
Network policies	
Anti-malware software	

Technique	Description
User access levels	
Firewalls	
Passwords	
Encryption	

1.7 Systems Software

1. What is the purpose of systems software? [2]

....

....

....

2. Give FOUR examples of operating systems. [4]

....

....

....

....

3. Describe three common features of an operating systems graphical user interface (GUI). [3]

Feature 1 ....

Feature 2 ....

Feature 3 ....

4. How does an operating system help to manage memory? [2]

....

....

....

....

5. Operating systems use multi-tasking. What is multi-tasking? [1]

....

....

....

....

6. If a computer is to print a document the operating system requires a printer driver. What is a

printer driver? [2]

....

....

....

7. (a) Explain how an operating system manages users? [1]

....

....

....

(b) Explain how does an operating system supports file management? [1]

....

....

....

8. (a) What is encryption utility software? [1]

....

....

....

(b) Explain, using an example, how encryption utility software might be used by a company. [2]

....

....

....

9. Explain what causes fragmentation of a mass storage device and how defragmentation can be used to alleviate this problem. [3]

....

....

....

....

....

10 (a) What is backup software? [2]

....

....

....

(b) Using an example, explain how backup software is used. [1]

....

....

....

....

(c) How does your school back up your files? [1]

....

....

....

(d) What is an incremental backup and what are the advantages of performing an incremental backup? [1]

....

....

....

1.8 Ethical, legal, cultural and environmental concerns

1. (a) What is meant by the term digital divide?

....

....

(b) Describe the impact of the digital divide on each of these groups. [4]

(i) People living on low incomes.

....

....

....

(ii) People living in remote locations far from urban centres.

....

....

....

(iii) Senior citizens with no experience of using technology.

....

....

....

(iv) People with disabilities

....

....

2. In the past a lot of personal data was stored on a person's home computer, whereas many people now store personal data online, using cloud storage. List two ethical questions that can be raised in relation to the storage of personal data moving from an individual computer to online, or cloud, storage? [2]

....

....

....

....

....

3. The way technology is being used within a family unit is changing. Describe two ways in which the use of technology has impacted on the culture of the family unit? [2]

....

....

....

....

....

4. A carbon footprint can be defined as: The total amount of greenhouse gases produced to directly and indirectly support human activities, usually expressed in tons of carbon dioxide (CO_2).

(a) Describe two ways in which the use of the Internet can contribute to a reduction in a teleworkers carbon footprint. [2]

....

....

....

....

....

(b) Describe how the increase in the use of cloud services can be harmful to the environment? [2]

....

....

....

....

....

5. In relation to the Data Protection Act (1998), list three of the rights of the data subject.[3]

1...

....

2...

....

3...

....

6. Which act of parliament protects the general public from the unauthorised access of computer materials? [1]

....

7. What two pieces of advice would you give someone to ensure that they are not prosecuted under the Copyright, Designs and Patents Act (1988)? [2]

1..

....

2..

....

8. What is a creative commons licence? [2]

....

....

....

....

....

9. Explain how the Freedom of Information Act (2000) can be of benefit to the general public. [1]

....

....

....

....

10. (a) What is open source software? [1]

....

....

....

(b) What is proprietary software? [1]

....

....

....

(c) What are the advantages and disadvantages of open source software and proprietary software for the consumer? [4]

Software Type	Advantages	Disadvantages
Open Source		
Proprietary		

2.1 Algorithms

1 (a) Match each word to the correct definition. [4]

1 **Algorithm**	**A** This involves filtering out (or ignoring) the characteristics that we don't need in order to concentrate on those that we do.

2 **Decompose**	**B** It involves breaking down a complex problem or system into smaller parts that are more manageable and easier to understand.

3 **Pattern Recognition**	**C** This is a list of rules to follow in order to solve a problem. The steps need to be in the right order.

4 **Abstraction**	**D** Once we have broken down a complex problem, it helps to examine the small problems for similarities. These similarities can help us to solve complex problems more efficiently.

(b) What is meant by the term Algorithmic Thinking? [2]

....

....

....

....

(c) Why is algorithmic thinking used in programming? [1]

....

....

....

....

2. (a) Use the list of words to complete this document. [7]

faster   linear   number   match   splits   tries   binary

A .... search starts at the beginning of the sequence of information and tries

to find a.................................... Once it has found a match it stops.

Another type of search is called a **..............................** **search**. This type of search

.... the parts of the list being searched into two with each check. This makes

it ....than a linear search. For example, if you were playing a number

guessing game and had to guess a .... between 1 and 10, it would not take more

than 3 ...., if you always choose the middle number each time and you were

told whether the number was higher or lower.

2 (b) This is an example of a binary search. It can be used to search for a particular student name.   Complete the algorithm by adding **T** for True and **F** for FALSE to the empty boxes. [6]

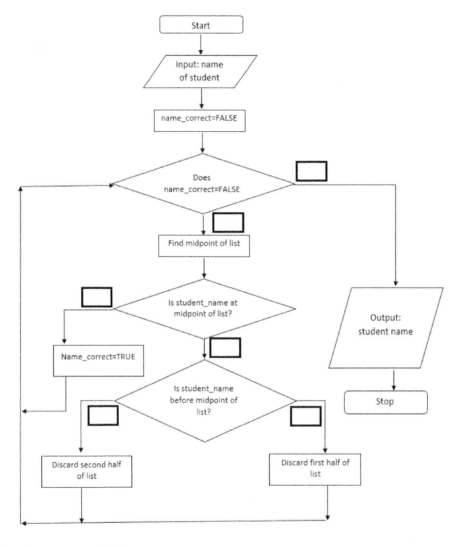

2 (c) What is a linear search? [3]

....

....

....

....

....

2 (d) Using pseudocode or a flow chart, write an algorithm for a linear search in the space provided below. [4]

3 There are some gaps in the bubble sort algorithm shown below.
Complete the gaps using the words shown. [6]

stop   next   swap   last   repeat   first

1. Look at the ………………………………….. number in the list.

2. Compare the current number with the next number.

3. Is the next number smaller than the current number?

    If so, ………………………………….the two numbers around. If not, do not swap.

4. Move to the ……………………………………. number along in the list and make

    this the current number.

5. Repeat from step 2 until the …………………………………………. number in the list has

    been reached.

6. If any numbers were swapped, …………………………………………. again from step 1.

7. If the end of the list is reached without any swaps being made, then the list is ordered

    and the algorithm can …………………………………………..

    4 (a) Explain the meaning of **merge sort**. [3]

    ………………………………………………………………………………………………………

    ………………………………………………………………………………………………………

    ………………………………………………………………………………………………………

    ………………………………………………………………………………………………………

    ………………………………………………………………………………………………………

    ………………………………………………………………………………………………………

(b) Give an advantage and a disadvantage of **merge sort** over a bubble or insertion sort.
[2]
Advantage...

....

....

Disadvantage...

....

....

5 (a) What is an insertion sort algorithm? [2]

....

....

....

....

....

(b) Is the insertion sort quicker or slower than the bubble sort? [1]

....

6. (a) Use pseudocode to create to produce an algorithm that asks for the length of a rectangle and the width of a rectangle. The algorithm then calculates the area of the square and displays a message "the area of the square is" and displays the area of the square. Include comments to explain what each line of code does. [8]

6(b) Use pseudocode to produce an algorithm that asks the person to enter a number between 1 and 20. If the number is greater or equal to 10 then display a message "The number is equal or higher than 10". However, if the number is less than 10 it should display the message **"The number is less than 10".** [5]

7 (a) Produce a flow chart that shows an algorithm for making a cup of tea. It should include: Sequence; Selection, Iteration. [5]

7(b) Produce a flow chart that inputs a random number and inputs the number that you want to guess. The flowchart then compares the number you have guessed with the random number and if they are the same you get a message to say "Correct", but if you guess incorrectly the algorithm uses an indefinite loop to allow the person to keep on guessing until they get the number right. [5]

7(c) If you wanted to give the person no more than three guesses, what would you need to add to the flowchart? [3]

....

....

....

....

2.2 Programming Techniques

1 (a) Define the following terms. [4]

Term	Definition
Variable	
Identifier	
Assignment	
Constant	

1 (b) This algorithm calculates the area of a circle in cm. [6]

```
rad=input("What is the radius of the circle?")

pi=3.14

area=pi*rad*^2

print("The area of the circle is",area)
```

i) Name two variables that can change when the program is run:

....

ii) Which identifier is a constant? ....

iii) If you assign the value of 1 to rad, what will the area be? ....

iv) Which variable provides input data for this program? ....

v) Which variable provides output data for this program? ....

2. (a) In the flow chart below identify sequence, selection and iteration. [3]

A is ....

B is ....

C is ....

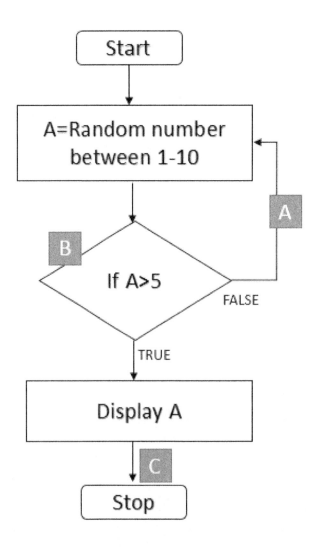

2 (b) In the Python Code below identify the **first line** where iteration and selection have been used. [2]

Iteration ……………………………………………….

Selection ……………………………………………….

1	def bubble_sort(list):
2	for n in range(len(list)-1,0,-1):
3	for i in range(n):
4	if list[i]>list[i+1]:
5	temp = list[i]
6	list[i] = list[i+1]
7	list[i+1] = temp
8	list = [54,26,93,17,77,31,44,55,20]
9	bubble_sort(list)
10	print(list)

3. Look at the pseudocode below. Write down what the program displays after it has been run. [2]

```
namePlace="Canada Water"

print(namePlace.length)

print(namePlace.substring(3,3))
```

………

4. (a) What does this program do? [1]

```
file1 = openRead("text.txt")

x = file1.readLine()

file1.close()
```

....

....

(b) What does this program do? [1]

```
file1 = openRead("text.txt")

while NOT file1.endOfFile()

print(file1.readLine())

endwhile file1.close()
```

....

....

(c)) What does this program do? [1]

```
file1 = openWrite("text.txt")

file1.writeLine("Canada Water")

file1.close()
```

....

....

5. Using the database table shown below. [4]

(a) How many **records** are there? .... How many **fields** are there? ....

(b) Give an example of a field name ………………………………………………….

(c) What would be a suitable datatype for the information in the **First Name** column?

…………………………………………..

First Name	Surname	Title	Gender	Date of Birth	Address	Town
Layla	Fong	Mrs	F	20/07/1982	27 Park Lane	Birmingham
Paige	Turner	Prof	F	14/12/1984	78 Manor Road	Chertsey
Americk	Patel	Dr	M	29/11/1981	14 York Avenue	York
Terry	McDougal	Dr	M	05/03/1975	19 South Avenue	London
Sam	Smith	Prof	M	07/11/1982	66 Park Road	Crediton
Mark	Smith	Prof	M	08/01/1954	38 The Lane	Worthing
Sarah	Scott	Miss	F	11/09/1990	76 Alexander Road	Burdon
Mark	Smith	Mr	M	20/02/1990	44 School Road	Tonbridge
Richard	Dean	Prof	M	08/08/1978	2 Main Road	Deeside
Bethany	Jones	Miss	F	07/04/1987	68 Cross Hand Road	Peterborough

6. (a) Complete the SQL database using the information shown in the Personal_info table below. The first two lines of code have been included to start you off. [4]

ID	First Name	Surname	Age	Post Code
1010	Aisha	Ahmed	15	E17 9PY
1011	Joanne	Strensky	14	E17 7TR
1012	Stephanie	Manley	15	E8 6RE
1013	Lucy	Grant	16	E10 9TS

CREATE TABLE Personal_Info

(ID int(4),

6 (b) Using the same table as 6 (a). What would be the result of the query shown below? [3]

Query:

SELECT Personal_info.First Name, Personal_info.Age FROM Personal_info ORDER BY Personal_Info.Age;

6 (c) Using the same table as 6 (a). What would be the result of the query shown below? [3]

Query:

SELECT Personal_Info.First Name, Personal_info.Surname, Personal_info.age,

FROM Personal_info WHERE ((Personal_info.age)>15);

6 (d) In the SQL language what is a wild card? Give an example of how a wild card could be used in SQL. [3]

....

....

....

6 (e) How will you add this data **1021, Jean, Johnson, 14,E9 1QY** to the personal_info database? [2]

ID	First Name	Surname	Age	Postcode
1010	Aisha	Ahmed	15	E17 9PY
1011	Joanne	Strensky	14	E17 7TR
1012	Stephanie	Manley	15	E8 6RE

6 (f) Lucy Grant has moved house and has the new post code **E17 6WS**. How would you update the database to show this new information? [3]

7 (a) What is the difference between a one dimensional array and a two dimensional array? [2]

....

....

....

....

7 (b) Below is a Python program that uses lists (arrays within Python are called lists). What would be the output from this program? [2]

```
names = ["Paul","Phillip","Paula","Phillipa"]
ages = [12,15,11,14]

print(names[0],"is",ages[0])
print(names[1],"is",ages[1])
print(names[2],"is",ages[2])
print(names[3],"is",ages[3])
```

7(c) The Python program below can be used to display data.

```
#Lists
list_radius=[]
list_circumference=[]
list_area=[]

#variables
pi=float(3.14)
circumference=float()
area=float()
no_rad=int()
radius=int()

#How many radii?
no_rad=int(input("How many radii do you want to enter into your table?"))
for n in range(no_rad):
    radius=n+1
    list_radius.append(radius)
    radius,circumference,area=n+1,2*pi*radius,pi*radius**2
    list_circumference.append(round(circumference,1))
    list_area.append(round(area,1))

print("Radius")
print(list_radius)
print("Circumference")
print(list_circumference)
print("Area")
print(list_area)
```

If the number of radii is 3 what will the program output? [4]

8(a) Programs often contain sub programs that perform particular tasks. Procedures and functions are both examples of sub programs. What is the difference between a function and a procedure? [1]

....

....

....

8 (b) What is meant by the term "call" a function? [1]

....

....

....

8 (c) What does this function do? [1]

function square(number)

return number^2

endfunction

....

....

9. (a) In relation to data types, what is meant by casting? [1]

....

....

....

9 (b) Complete the table below, for each item choose an appropriate data type. [8]

Item	Data Type
Surname	
Telephone number	
Is the sensor detecting light?	
Number of people in a car	
Value of Pi to two decimal places	
Postcode	
Is the circuit open or closed?	
Population of greenfly	

10 (a) Provide an example of how each of these arithmetic operators are used, if x=20 y=6. The first one has been done for you. [6]

Arithmetic Operators	Example of use using x=20 y=6
+	x+y=26
-	
*	
/	

MOD	
DIV	
^	

10 (b) What will be the output from each of the calculations shown below? [6]

(i) 14 MOD 5 ....

(ii) 20 MOD 10 ....

(iii)100 MOD 11 ....

(iv) 14 DIV 5 ....

(v) 20 DIV 10 ....

(vi)100 DIV 11 ....

11. (a) What will be the output from the algorithms below? [3]

num1=4   num2=8

Pseudocode	Output

If num1>num2 then
    print ("yes")
else
    print("no")
endif	

If num1!=num2*4 then
    print ("yes")
else
    print("no")
endif	

If num1*9>=num2^5 then
    print ("yes")
else
    print("no")
endif	

11 (b) What will be the output from the algorithms below? [4]

num1=10   num2=8   num3=15

Pseudocode	Output

If num1>num2 AND (num2-num1)>1 then
    print ("yes")
else
    print("no")
endif
	no

If num3*2=num1*3 OR num3>(num2+num1) then
    print ("yes")
else
    print("no")
endif
	yes

If num2*12>=num1^2 OR num3!=num2*2 then
    print ("yes")
else
    print("no")
endif
	yes

If NOT num3*5<=num1^3 AND num1<=num2*2 then
    print ("yes")
else
    print("no")
endif
	no

2.3 Producing Robust Programs

1 (a) In terms of computer programming, what is meant by defensive design and why is it used? [2]

....

....

....

1(b) The table below is about types of defensive design. Complete the table. [10]

Term	Definition	Example
Validation		
Sanitization		
Planning for contingencies		

Anticipating misuse		
Authentication		

2 A common defence strategy is to ensure that code is written in such a way that other programmers can understand it. This is called maintainability and it reduces the chance of coding mistakes or bugs. Describe two ways in which code can be made more maintainable. [2]

1..

2..

3 (a) In computer programming, why is it important that programs are tested? [1]

....

....

3 (b) Complete the table below. [2]

Types of testing	Explanation
	Testing is ongoing throughout the development process. You may code an aspect of your program and test it before moving on.
	This is carried out at the end of the development process, when the program is complete, the program should be tested again (as a whole) against the requirements of the user to ensure their needs have been met.

4. (a) Fill in the gaps below using the words shown. [6]

logic   programming   unexpected   syntax   translated   convert

A .... error is simply an error where the code written doesn't meet the

rules of the .... language.

These errors appear when the source code is ....into machine code.

The translator tries to ....the code, but if the code doesn't meet the

rules of the translator, it throws up an error.

A ....error is one where the code is written in accordance with the

programming rules and is therefore translated and runs, however, the program produces

....results.

4(b) Circle the syntax errors in the Python program shown below. [2]

```
import turtle
def sq():
    for n in range(4)
        turtle.forward(100)
        turtle.right(90
sq()
```

4(c) Circle the syntax errors in the Python program shown below. [3]

```
def ask(q,c):
    answer=input(q)
    if answer=c:
        print(Correct!)
ask("What is 2+2?","4")
```

5(a) What is the logic error in this Python program used to calculate the sum of two numbers? [1]

```
x=input("What is your first number?: ")
y=input("What is your second number?: ")
sum=x+y
print("The sum of your first and second number is",sum)

What is your first number?: 2
What is your second number?: 2
The sum of your first and second number is 22
>>>
```

....

....

5 (b) What is the logic error in this Python program used to find out the average of two numbers? [1]

```
x = 13
y = 8
average = x + y / 2
print("The average is",average)

The average is 17.0
>>>
```

....

....

6 (a) Describe the following types of test data and given an example for each. [6]

Type of test data	Description	Example
Valid Data (Normal)		
Invalid Data (Erroneous)		
Borderline Data		

6(b) List four things that must be included in a test plan. [4]

1..

2..

3..

4..

2.4 Computational Logic

1 (a) Explain what is meant by **binary**? [1]

....

....

1 (b) Why is data represented in computer systems in binary form? [1]

....

....

....

2 (a) A NOT gate has just one input. The output of the circuit will be the opposite of the input. Complete the table below to show what happens to the inputs. [2]

Input	Output
1	
0	

2(b) An **AND** gate can be used on a gate with two inputs. Complete the truth table below to show the output from an AND Gate. [4]

Input A	Input B	Output
0	0	
0	1	
1	0	
1	1	

2(c) The **OR** gate has two inputs. Complete the truth table below to show the output from an AND Gate. [4]

Input A	Input B	Output
0	0	
0	1	
1	0	
1	1	

3 (a) Look at this Venn diagram, which shows the number of children who take part in two sports in year 7 and then fill in the gaps below. [3]

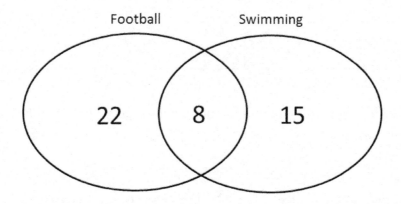

(i) There were ……… children who took part in football **AND** swimming.

(ii) There were ……… children who took part in football but **NOT** swimming.

(iii) There were 15 children who took part in swimming …………………… football.

(iv) There were ……… children who took part in football OR swimming.

3 (b)   Determine the output for each of the examples below, by assigning the following values to the variables.

x=10 y=20 z=15

Question	Pseudocode	Output

(i)	if x>y AND z>y then
	print("true")
	else
	print("false")
	endif	

(ii)	if x==y OR z<y then
	print("true")
	else
	print("false")
	endif	

(iii)	if NOT(x>y) OR x==y/2 then
	print("tru")
	else
	print("false")
	endif	

4(a) A jewellery shop has an alarm system that they are turn on at night that has a sensor on the door and a sensor on the window. The alarm will go off if someone tries to enter the shop via the door OR the window.

Complete the truth table below to show how Boolean logic is used. [4]

Door opened	Window opened	Alarm sounds
T		
T		
F		
F		

4(b) Create a truth table for the following pseudocode. [4]

if NOT (X == 6 OR Y == 12) then
    print ("true")
 endif

X	Y	NOT(X OR Y)
T	T	
F	T	
T	F	
F	F	

5 (a) A farmer grows her tomatoes in poly-tunnels. She has decided to set up an automatic watering system.

At the entrance to the poly-tunnels there is a light sensor, and inside the poly-tunnel within the soil there is a moisture sensor. The farmer only wants the watering system to turn on at night and only when the soil is dry. The farmer chooses to use two **NOT** gates and one **AND** gate.

Draw a diagram to show the logic gate structure used in the poly-tunnel. [2]

5 (b) (i) A logic circuit can be written as **Q = (NOT A) OR B**:

Draw the logic gate in the space below. [3]

5(b)(ii) Complete the truth table for the logic gate structure shown in 5(b)(i). [4]

Input		Output
A	**B**	**Q**
0	0	
0	1	
1	0	
1	1	

6 (a) MOD and DIV are arithmetic operators. Explain the difference between them. [2]

....

....

....

....

....

6(b) What would be the output produced in each of the examples of pseudocode shown below? [8]

	Pseudocode	Output
(i)	a=7 b=14 c=12 print(a*b) +(c*a)	
(ii)	a=7 b=20 c=12 print(a+c+(a^4)) +(b*a)	

(iii)	a=6
	b=14
	c=12
	if a<=b then
	print(a*b) +(c/a)
	else
	print(a+b)-c^6
	endif	

(iv)	a=5
	b=14
	c=12
	if a>=b OR c/2>=7 then
	print(cMODa)
	else
	print(cDIVa)	

2.5 Translators and facilities of languages

1(a) List three things that programming languages have the ability to do. [3]

....

....

....

....

....

....

1(b) What is the difference between a high-level and a low-level programming language? [6]

High-Level	Low-Level

1(c) Produce a list of THREE high level programming languages. [3]

1 ....

2 ....

3 ....

2 In computer science, what is the purpose of a translator? [3]

....

....

....

....

....

3(a) What is an assembly language? [1]

....

....

....

3(b) Explain the purpose of an assembler. [2]

....

....

....

....

4 Complete this table in relation to the characteristics of a compiler and an interpreter. [10]

	Compiler	Interpreter
Function		
Error checking		
Speed		
Examples		
Use		

5 (a) What is an Integrated Development Environment (IDE)? [1]

....

....

5(b) (i) What is the role played by an **editor** in an IDE? [2]

....

....

....

5(b) (ii) The **editor** has features that assist with the writing and editing of code. Explain these

features below. [3]

Feature	Explanation
Auto-completion	
Bracket matching	
Syntax checks	

5(c) What is a **run-time environment**? Why is this important? [2]

....

....

....

....

....

2.6 Data representation

1(a) Place the following terms in order according to size with the smallest at the top of the table. [2]

Kilobyte, terabyte, nibble, petabyte, byte, gigabyte, megabyte, bit

1(b) (i) Using the binary system, how many **bytes** are there in a Kilobyte? [1]

....

1(b) (ii) Using the binary system, how many **bits** are there in a Kilobyte? [1]

....

1(c) Based on the binary system, convert the following values that represent file sizes into **bits** and show your working. [6]

(i) 8 kB

....

....

(ii) 290 kB

....

....

(iii) 3 MB

....

....

2 Why does data need to be converted into binary format to be processed by a computer? [2]

....

....

....

....

3 (a) Convert the following denary whole numbers into 8 bit binary numbers. [4]

(i) 10

....

(ii) 27

....

(iii) 100

....

(iv) 232

....

3(b) Convert the following binary numbers into denary whole numbers. [4]

(i) 00101010

....

(ii) 00001000

....

(iii) 10010011

....

(iv) 10111100

....

4(a) Add the following 8 bit binary integers. [4]

(i) 00001010 + 00001000

....

(ii) 01001001 + 00110011

....

(iii) 00010011 + 00000111

....

(iv) 10111100 +10000001

....

4(b) Using a suitable example explain overflow errors. [2]

....

....

....

5 (a) Convert the following denary whole numbers into two digit hexadecimals and show your working. [8]

(i) 111

....

....

(ii) 108

....

....

 (iii) 129

....

....

 (iv) 244

....

....

5 (b) Convert the following two digit hexadecimals into denary whole numbers and show your working. [8]

(i) 8A

....

....

(ii) 62

....

....

(iii) F1

....

....

(iv) 9A

....

....

6 (a) Convert the following binary numbers into two digit hexadecimals and show your working. [8]

(i) 01010101

....

(ii) 10001111

....

....

(iii) 00011110

....

....

(iv) 11111110

....

....

6 (b) Convert the following two digit hexadecimals into binary numbers and show your working. [8]

(i) 6B

....

....

(ii) 89

....

....

(iii) BB

....

....

(iv) 1D

....

....

7 Explain, using an example, the meaning of the term "check digit". [2]

....

....

....

....

8 (a) What is the ASCII character set and how is it used? [2]

....

....

....

....

8(b) What is the advantage of using extended ASCII? [1]

....

....

....

....

8(c) What is the **Unicode** character set and why is it used? [2]

....

....

....

....

9(a) What is a pixel? [1]

....

....

9(b) If one bit is used for each pixel in an image, how many colours can be represented in the

image? [1]

....

9(c) If one nibble is used for each pixel in an image, how many colours can be represented in the image? [1]

....

9(d) A HD TV has a 30 bit colour depth - How many colours is this? [1]

....

10 List FOUR examples of metadata that can be stored with a photograph. [4]

....

....

....

....

11 (a) Fill in the gaps below using the words provided. [6]

bits bytes data uploaded speed transmitted

Data is transmitted across the internet as .... (0s and 1s) and the ....is measured as bits per second. The more bits that are .... per second the faster the internet connection. How long it takes to send a file to a mobile phone over a 4G network is determined by the bandwidth. Bandwidth is a measure of how quickly ....can be downloaded or .... It is usually measured as bits per second (bps) or megabits per second (mbps). File sizes are measured in .... (B) rather than bits (b).

11(b) Answer the questions below.

(i) What piece of equipment is needed to record sound?

………………………………………………………………………………………

(ii) Once the sound has been recorded, what is it converted into so that it can be used on a computer?

………………………………………………………………………………………

(iii) In relation to digital audio, what is meant by **bit rate**? [1]

………………………………………………………………………………………

………………………………………………………………………………………

………………………………………………………………………………………

(iv) In relation to digital audio, what is meant by **sampling frequency**? [1]

………………………………………………………………………………………

………………………………………………………………………………………

………………………………………………………………………………………

(v) If fewer samples are taken, what usually happens to the quality of the sound recording? [1]

………………………………………………………………………………………

………………………………………………………………………………………

………………………………………………………………………………………

12(a) Sound and image files are often compressed. Explain what is meant by compression? [1]

………………………………………………………………………………………

………………………………………………………………………………………

………………………………………………………………………………………

12(b) In relation to viewing video files on a computer, why is compression important? [2]

....

....

....

12 (c) What is the difference between **lossy** and **lossless** compression? [2]

....

....

....

Question Number	1.1 Systems Architecture - Mark Scheme	Mark
1 a	It is the "brain" of the computer [1 mark] It interprets/executes/processes program instructions. [1 mark]	**2**
1 b	The control unit directs the operation of the processor. [1 mark] **It tells the computer's memory, arithmetic/logic unit and input and output devices how to respond to a program's instructions.**	**1**
1 c	It is used to perform arithmetic [1 mark] and logic operations [1 mark] within the CPU.	**2**
1 d	A cache used by the CPU to reduce the average time to access data from the main memory. [1 mark] Therefore allowing the CPU to process data more quickly.[1 mark] **The cache is a smaller, faster memory which stores copies of the data from frequently used main memory locations.**	**2**
1 e	Factor: Clock speed. [1 mark] The more instructions that are processed each second the faster the CPU. [1 mark] Factor: Number of cores. [1 mark] By putting more cores in a chip you can get more processing done at the same time, therefore improving CPU performance. [1 mark]	**4**
2 a	The Memory Address Register (MAR) is a register that **stores** the memory address from which data will be fetched to the CPU or the address to which data will be sent and stored. [2 marks]	**2**
2 b	The Memory Data Register (MDR) is the register of a computer's control unit that contains the **data** to be stored in the computer storage(e.g. RAM), or the data after a fetch from the computer storage. [2 marks]	**2**
2 c	A program counter is a register in a computer processor that contains the address (location) of the instruction being executed at the current time. [1 mark] As each instruction gets fetched, the program counter increases its stored value by 1. [1 mark] After each instruction is fetched, the program counter points to the next instruction in the sequence. [1 mark]	**3**
2 d	The accumulator is a register in which arithmetic and logic results are stored. [1 mark] Preventing the need to write the results of each calculation to main memory. [1 mark]	**2**
3 a	e.g. - Digital Camera - Smoke detector - Microwave Oven	**1**

3 b	Purpose relates to device chosen. E.g. a smoke detector detects smoke and a speaker emits an alarm. Components linked to purpose. E.g. • Power Supply • Processor • Memory • Timers • Serial communication ports • Input/Output circuits • Sensors	3
3 c	e.g. • Digital Camera • Smoke detector • Microwave Oven	1
3 d	Purpose relates to device chosen. E.g. a smoke detector detects smoke and a speaker emits an alarm. Components linked to purpose. E.g. • Power Supply • Processor • Memory • Timers • Serial communication ports • Input/Output circuits • Sensors	3

Question Number	1.2 Memory - Mark Scheme	Mark
1	a. Random Access Memory. [1 mark] b. Read Only Memory. [1 mark] c. This is a form of data storage. [1 mark] d. RAM allows the computer to read data quickly [1 mark] to run applications. [1 mark] e. It is mainly used to store firmware [1 mark] and contains the programming required to boot up a device.[1 mark] f. RAM is volatile [1 mark] and when the device is powered off the data held in RAM is lost. [1 mark] g. ROM is non-volatile [1 mark] and when the device is powered off the data held in ROM is not lost.[1 mark]	9
2 a	• Allows you to setup your computer system [1 mark] • Test the hardware to make sure there are no errors before the operating system is loaded [1 mark] • Locate the operating system and pass control to it [1 mark]	2
2b	• Tablet [1mark] • Smart Phone [1 mark] • Games Console [1 mark]	2
3 a	• When a program is running, calculations are performed using information stored in RAM [1 mark] • It is used to store information input by a user. [1 mark]	2

	• While a user edits a document its text and formatting information is stored temporarily in RAM [1 mark]	
3b	• Tablet [1 mark] • Smart Phone [1 mark] • Games Console [1 mark]	2
4 a	Sometimes the RAM memory is low on space [1 mark] and so the computer creates a section of volatile memory on the storage drive (e.g. Hard Disk Drive)[1 mark] It does this when the computer is running many processes and the RAM is low on space [1 mark]	3
4 b	Virtual memory is much slower than RAM [1 mark] because data needs to be transferred backwards and forwards rather than just executing the instruction [1 mark]	2
5 a	Flash memory is a type of non-volatile memory -when it is powered off it retains the information [1 mark] Data is stored in units called blocks [1 mark]	2
5 b	• Smart Phone.[1 mark] • Tablet [1 mark] • Laptops [1 mark]	2
5 c	• Takes up less space [1 mark] • Solid State – therefore more mobile [1 mark] • Fast transfer of data [1 mark]	2
5 d	Cheaper cost [1 mark] Generally have a larger storage capacity [1 mark]	2

Question Number	1.3 Storage - Mark Scheme	Mark
1 a	Secondary storage is non-volatile storage [1] that is not under the direct control of a computer's central processing unit (CPU) [1].	2
1 b	• Internal Hard Disk Drive [1] • External Hard Disk Drive [1] • Optical Drive [1] • Solid State Drive (Flash Drive) [1] Max 2 marks	2
1 c	The computer needs somewhere to store the operating system, software and data files when the computer is powered off [1] as primary storage is volatile and therefore is incapable of performing this task.[1]	2
2 a	• DVD Drive –4.7 GB • Solid State Drive – 4GB –to 256 GB • USB Memory Stick – 2 to 64 GB • BluRay Drive – 50 GB	4
2 b	• 1560 KB x 45 = 371200 KB = 371.2 MB • 650 MB x 15 = 9750 MB	3

	• 9750 MB + 371.2 MB = 10121.2 MB = 10.12 GB • [1 mark] • She requires a 16 [1 mark] GB [1 mark]USB Memory Stick	
3	Optical Drive **Advantages** • Data stored on optical media is light and easily transported. • Fairly durable and reliable form of data storage. **Disadvantages** • Storage capacity fairly small in comparison with other storage devices (between 700 MB and 50 GB) • Fairly slow data transfer speeds 72 megabits per second. • Media can be damaged if mishandled. Magnetic **Advantages** • Large storage capacity – 2 TB • Data transfer speeds faster than an optical drive approx. 140 megabits per second. • Low cost **Disadvantages** • They have moving parts and if they are dropped they can easily be damaged. • They are larger than Solid State Drives and therefore cannot be used in small devices e.g. a smart phone. Solid State Drive **Advantages** • They have no moving parts • Very small making them ideal for portable devices. • Silent **Disadvantages** • More expensive in comparison with magnetic and optical drives. • Generally smaller storage capacity than magnetic drives.	6
4 a	Most Suitable storage device - Optical storage [1 mark] Why – • Because Joe can copy the music onto CDs, which are low cost, and send them through the post • He doesn't need a huge storage capacity • CDs are robust and not easily damaged [2 marks]	3
4 b	Most Suitable storage device - SSD [1 mark] Why • There are no moving parts in a flash drive therefore it is portable • It has a fast boot up time. [2 marks]	3

4 c	Most Suitable storage device - Magnetic Drive [1 mark] Why • Large capacity eg 2TB • Easily accessed. • Doesn't need to be portable. [2 marks]	3

Question Number	1.4 Wired and wireless networks - Mark Scheme	Mark
1 a	A local area network (LAN) is a group of computers and associated peripheral devices [1] connected to a server [1] within a small geographic area such as an office building or home.[1]	2
1 b	School/ any organisation that has networked computers on a single site or building.	1
2 a	A wide area network (WAN) is a network that is dispersed over a large geographical area [1]. It typically consists of two or more LANS [1] that have been connected together through public networks [1]	2
2 b	Government department/ any organisation that has networked computers over a number of geographically separated sites or buildings.[1]	1
3 a	Latency is the amount of time [1] a packet of data [1] takes to get from one point in the network to another [1].	2
3 b	If a network has low latency then the delay [1] between an input being processed and an output being produced is so fast that it is unperceived by humans[1] E.g. When you make a VOIP call/Financial Markets [1]	3
4	How quickly data can be transferred across a network. [1] As bandwidth increases, more information per unit of time can pass through the network.[1]	2
5 a	When a data packet that is sent never arrives at its destination [1]	1
5 b	Glitches, errors, or network overloading [1]	1
5 c	Data packets are retransmitted [1]	1
6 a	Server connected to hub/switch [1] PC(s) connected to hub/switch [1] Network printer connected to hub/switch [1]	3
6 b	**Advantages** • Network peripherals e.g. printers are controlled centrally [1] • Backups and network security can be controlled centrally [1] • Users can access shared data which is controlled centrally [1] • Software licences and installation for each workstation can be controlled centrally [1]	4

	Disadvantages • The server can be expensive to purchase [1] • Specialist staff such as a network manager is often needed [1] • If key parts of the network fails such as the server or the switch, a lot of disruption can occur at the client end [1]	
7 a	No Server [1] PC(s) connected to hub/switch [1] Laptop connects to wireless access point to hub/switch [1]	3
7 b	Advantages • No need for a network operating system • Does not need an expensive server because individual workstations are used to access the files • No need for specialist staff such as network technicians because each user sets their own permissions as to which files they are willing to share. • Much easier to set up than a client-server network - does not need specialist knowledge • If one computer fails it will not disrupt any other part of the network. It just means that those files aren't available to other users at that time. • Peer to Peer can also be set up across the internet, where the internet is effectively acting as a hub. There can be thousands of computers within such a network. Disadvantages • Because each computer might be being accessed by others it can slow down the performance for the user • Files and folders cannot be centrally backed up • Files and resources are not centrally organised into a specific 'shared area'. They are stored on individual computers and might be difficult to locate if the computer's owner doesn't have a logical filing system. • Ensuring that viruses are not introduced to the network is the responsibility of each individual user • Although it is often the case that a password protected user account is set up on a machine, this does not have to be the case and so security is not as robust as a client server model. • Setting up a peer to peer network over the internet from scratch is highly technical and requires serious expertise, but actually joining an already set-up peer to peer network is relatively simple.	4
8	1 B 2 D 3 E 4 A 5 C	3
9 a	Domain Name Servers (DNS) are the Internet's equivalent of a phone book. They maintain a directory of domain names [1] and translate them to Internet Protocol (IP) addresses. [1]	2
9 b	This is necessary because, although domain names are easy for people to remember, computers or machines, access websites based on IP addresses. [1]	1
9 c	The term "host" means any computer that has full two-way access to other computers on the Internet. [1] A host has a specific "local or host number" that, together with the network number, forms its unique IP address. [1]	1
9 d	The practice of using a network of remote servers [1] hosted on the Internet to store, manage, and process data, [1] rather than a local server or a personal computer. [1]	2

10 a	VPN, or virtual private network, is a network that is constructed by using public wires — usually the Internet [1] — to connect to a private network, such as a company's internal network. [1]	2
10 b	Workers can connect to their company's network from home. [1]	1

Question Number	1.5 Network topologies, protocols and layers - Mark Scheme	Mark
1 a	In networks, a topology is a diagram that shows the arrangement of a network [1], including its nodes and connecting lines [1].	2
1 b	Diagram to show: Star network topology- there is a central computer/hub or server to which all the workstations are connected. [1] Mesh network topology - every node has a connection to every other node in the network.[1]	2
1 c	Star Network **Advantages [1]** • Inexpensive • Easy to install, wire and maintain • Easier to detect faults • If a workstation is removed or faulty this does not affect other nodes. **Disadvantages [1]** • If the switch/hub fails the network cannot function Mesh Network **Advantages [1]** • Does not require switch/hub • Extremely tolerant when network is damaged **Disadvantages [1]** • Difficult to set up • Expensive to maintain and trouble shoot	4
2 a	WiFi is a technology that uses **radio** waves to provide network connectivity. Wifi provides **wireless** connectivity to your devices by emitting a **frequency** between 2.4 and 5GHz In radio waves the **higher** the frequency the **shorter** the range	5

2 b			2.4 GHz	5 GHz		6
		Network Range	Wider Range [1]	Shorter Range [1]		
		Interference	Higher[1]	Lower[1]		
		Use for home network	Recommended for simple internet browsing [1]	Recommended for media streaming [1]		

2 c	Wireless Encryption - encrypts the messages that are sent between your computer's wireless network adapter [1] and the wireless router. [1]	2
2 d	Wireless Encryption prevents unknown computers from gaining access to your network. [1]	1
3	A network that uses **Ethernet** cables to connect network devices on a LAN. [1]	1
4 a	Network protocols are formal standards and policies comprised of rules, procedures and formats [1] that define communication between two or more devices over a network. [1]	2
4 b	1 TCP/IP (Transmission Control Protocol/Internet Protocol) [1] 2 HTTP (Hyper Text Transfer Protocol) [1] 3 HTTPS (Hyper Text Transfer Protocol Secure) [1] 4 FTP (File Transfer Protocol) [1] 5 POP (Post Office Protocol) [1] 6 IMAP (Internet Message Access Protocol) [1] 7 SMTP (Simple Mail Transfer Protocol) [1]	7
5	It is a mode of data transmission in which a message is broken into a number of parts [1] which are sent independently [1 and reassembled at the destination.[1]	3

Question Number	1.6 System security - Mark Scheme	Mark
1 a	Malware is short for "malicious software," malware refers to software programs designed to damage or do other unwanted actions on a computer system. [1]	1
1 b	Examples: viruses, worms, Trojan horses, and spyware. Viruses are self-replicating computer programs which install themselves without user consent. They often perform some type of harmful activity on the infected host device. A computer worm is a standalone malware computer program that replicates itself in order to spread to other computers. Often, it uses a computer network to spread itself, relying on security failures on the target computer to access it. Trojan horses do not replicate themselves but they can be just as destructive. One type of Trojan horse is a program that claims to rid your computer of viruses but instead introduces viruses onto your computer. Spyware is software that enables a user to obtain covert information about another's computer activities by transmitting data covertly from their hard drive.	6
2	General greeting [1] Link not to expected domain [1]	3

	Requests personal information [1] Suggests a sense of urgency. [1]	
3 a	Psychological manipulation of people into performing actions or divulging confidential information [1]	1
3 b	Pretend you work at a company and get access to the network on a workstation that is already logged in. [1] Gaining network information from existing employees. [1] Gather personal information about a worker and use this to identify their password. [1]	1
3 c	A Brute force attack is a trial and error method [1] used to decode encrypted data such as passwords, through trying every possible combination in sequence [1] until you arrive at the correct password.	2
3 d	A denial-of-service (DoS) attack is an attempt to make a machine or network resource unavailable to its intended users. [1] This could be to extort money or for political reasons. [1]	2
3 e	A data interception occurs when packets of data travel across a network, they are susceptible to being read, altered, or "hijacked." [1] Hijacking occurs when a hostile party intercepts network traffic and poses as one of the session endpoints. An attacker can easily read all text traffic. [1]	2
3 f	SQL injection attack is used on database applications [1] Malicious SQL statements are inserted into an entry field for execution [1] transmitting the data to the hacker. [1]	2
4 a	Acceptable Use Policy – This tells company employees how they should behave when using the network. [1] This is a signed agreement that employees are bound by. [1] Ensures that employees follow the network rules supplied by their employer. [1]	2
4 b	**Penetration testing** Penetration testing is the practice of testing a computer system, network or Web application to find vulnerabilities that an attacker could exploit. [1] **Network forensics** Network forensics relates to the monitoring and analysis of computer network traffic for the purposes of information gathering, legal evidence, or intrusion detection. [1] **Network policies** A network security policy is a document that outlines rules for computer network access. [1] **Anti-malware software** Anti-malware software protects against infections caused by many types of malware. [1] **Firewalls**	8

Firewalls limit access of unauthorised users to your computer and network. [1] **User access levels** Network managers can set up groups of users with different levels of access to the network. [1] **Passwords** A password is a sequence of characters used to determine that a computer user requesting access to a computer system is really that particular user. [1] **Encryption**. Encryption is the conversion of electronic data into another coded form, called cipher text [1], which cannot be easily understood by anyone except authorised users.[1] max 1	

Question Number	1.7 Systems Software - Mark Scheme	Mark
1	System software forms an interface between software applications, such as a word processing program or an Internet browser [1], and computer hardware, including peripherals such as printers.[1]	2
2	• Microsoft Windows 10 [1] • Linux [1] • OS X [1] • iOS [1] • Android [1]	4
3	• Windows [1] • Icons [1] • Menus [1] • Pointer [1]	3
4	• It helps to keep track of each and every memory location [1] • It checks how much memory is to be allocated to processes. [1] • It decides which process will get memory at what time. [1] • It transfers programs into and out of memory [1] allocates free space between programs [1] • keeps track of memory usage [1]	2
5	Multi-tasking is performing multiple tasks (processes) over a certain period of time by executing them concurrently. [1]	1
6	A program that controls the operations of a printer. [1] Whenever you print a document, the printer driver feeds data to the printer with the correct control commands. [1]	2
7 a	Operating systems can manage users, providing individualised, secure accounts for each user. [1]	1
7 b	Creates a file system to organise files and directories [1]	1
8 a	Encryption utility software is system software designed to encrypt data on a computer. [1]	1
8 b	Encryption utility software might be used by a company to prevent third parties from viewing any of the original data. [1]	2

	This is particularly important for sensitive data like social security numbers. [1]	
9	The files on a hard drive often becomes fragmented i.e. in non-contiguous locations. [1] Defragmentation is a process that reduces the amount of fragmentation. [1] It does this by physically organizing the contents of the mass storage device used to store files into the smallest number of contiguous regions (fragments).[1]	2
10 a	Backup software is a computer program used to create exact copies of files, databases or entire computers. [1] These programs may later use to restore the original contents in the event of data loss.[1]	2
10 b	Any reasonable example [1]	1
10 c	Any reasonable example [1]	1
10 d	A security copy which contains only those files which have been altered since the last full backup. [1]	1

Question Number	1.8 Ethical, legal, cultural and environmental concerns - Mark Scheme	Mark
1 a	The gulf between those who have ready access to computers and the Internet, and those who do not. [1]	1
1 b i	Cannot afford to pay for technology [1]	1
1 b ii	Less access to broadband internet [1]	1
1 b iii	Harder for older people who are 'offline' to access vital services and could deter people from seeking the support they need. [1]	1
1 b iv	Devices not always designed to suit the needs of people with disabilities. [1]	1
2	<ul><li>Who owns the data? [1]</li><li>Where is the data stored? [1]</li><li>Who has access to the data? [1]</li><li>Who has access to the metadata? [1]</li><li>Which countries laws apply to the protection of this data? [1]</li></ul>	2
3	Families have opportunities for more regular communications via smart phones and other devices. [1] In the past there was a need to share a single device e.g. TV and watching TV was a shared experience but now every individual within a household can access media on their own device. [1] Parents have lost control over how their children communicate with their friends. [1]	2
4 a	Teleworkers can use the internet to send emails rather than post letters therefore no delivery vehicles required. [1] Teleworkers do not need to physically travel to work therefore reducing their carbon footprint. [1] Teleworkers do not need to attend meetings as they can instead use video conference software. [1]	2

	Teleworkers do not need to print off files and so there is a reduction in paper usage. [1] The employer does not need to provide the electricity and lighting for their employee. [1]	
4 b	The growth in the number and size of data centres is an issue. [1] Data centres require large amounts of electricity to power the servers and they also need to power air conditioning units to cool down the servers. [1] Technology uses 10% of the world's energy. [1]	2
5	• a right of access to a copy of the information comprised in their personal data. [1] • a right to object to processing that is likely to cause or is causing damage or distress. [1] • a right to prevent processing for direct marketing. [1] • a right to object to decisions being taken by automated means. [1] • a right in certain circumstances to have inaccurate personal data rectified, blocked, erased or destroyed. [1] • a right to claim compensation for damages caused by a breach of the Act. [1]	3
6	The Computer Misuse Act (1990) [1]	1
7	Do not do anything without the permission of the copyright holder. [1] Do not copy the work. [1] Do not rent, lend or issue copies of the work to the public. [1] Do not perform, broadcast or show the work in public. [1]	2
8	A Creative Commons license enable the free distribution of copyrighted work. [1] It is used when an author wants to give people the right to share, use, and build upon a work that they have created. [1]	2
9	The Freedom of Information Act 2000 creates a public "right of access" to information held by public authorities. [1].	1
10 a	Open source software is free and openly available to everyone. [1] People who create open source products publish the code and allow others to use and modify it. [1]	1
10 b	Proprietary software is software that legally remains the property of the organisation, group, or individual who created it. [1] The organisation that owns the rights to the product usually does not release the source code, and may insist that only those who have purchased a special licence key can use it. [1]	1
10 c	<u>Open Source</u> **Advantages** • Can be copied [1] • Usually free [1] • Can be modified [1] **Disadvantages**	4

	• Not always maintained and developed [1] • Can be unreliable [1] Proprietary Software **Advantages** • Well maintained [1] • New features developed [1] **Disadvantages** • You usually need to pay [1] • Cannot be modified – no access to source code.[1]	

Question Number	2.1 Algorithms - Mark Scheme	Mark
1 a	1-C; 2-B; 3-D; 4-A	4
1 b	Algorithmic thinking is a way of finding a solution to a problem [1] through the clear definition of the steps needed.[1]	2
1 c	It is possible to use algorithmic thinking to: • produce solutions that can be automated [1] • remove the need for human intervention. [1]	1
2 a	A **linear** search starts at the beginning of the sequence of information and tries to find a **match**. Once it has found a match it stops. Another type of search is called a **binary search.** This type of search **splits** the parts of the list being searched into two with each check. This makes it **faster** than a linear search. For example, if you were playing a number guessing game and had to guess a **number** between 1 and 10, it would not take more than 3 **tries**, if you always choose the middle number each time and you were told whether the number was higher or lower.	7
2 b		6

2 c	A linear search is a sequential search. [1] It starts at the beginning of the list and moves through the items one by one [1], until it finds a matching value or reaches the end without finding one [1].	3
2 d	Algorithm includes: Selection: Compare item with the data you are looking for [1] If they are the same then stop [1] If they are not the same move on to next item [1] Loop: Repeat steps above [1]	4
3	1 first 3 swap 4 next 5 last 6 repeat 7 stop	7
4 a	The merge sort repeatedly divides [1] a list into two smaller lists [1] until the size of the list becomes one [1] The individual lists are then merged.[1] Max 3 marks	3
4 b	Advantage – more efficient [1] and faster [1] than bubble or insertion sort. Max 1 Disadvantage – complex to code [1]	2
5 a	Examines each item in turn [1] Inserts it in the correct position within the list. [1]	2
5 b	Quicker [1]	1
6 a	length = input ("Please enter the length")[1] //Ask the user for the length of the rectangle. [1] width = input ("Please enter the width")[1] //Ask the user for the width of the rectangle. [1] area = length * width [1] //Find the area by multiplying the length by the width. [1] print ("The area of the square is: "+ area)[1] //output the area. [1]	8

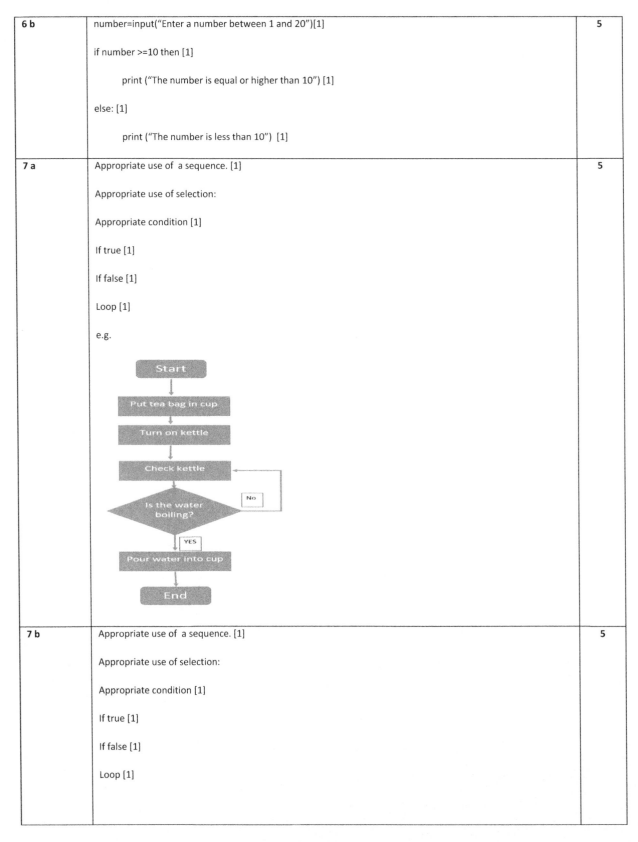

6 b	number=input("Enter a number between 1 and 20")[1]	5
	if number >=10 then [1]	
	print ("The number is equal or higher than 10") [1]	
	else: [1]	
	print ("The number is less than 10") [1]	
7 a	Appropriate use of a sequence. [1]	5
	Appropriate use of selection:	
	Appropriate condition [1]	
	If true [1]	
	If false [1]	
	Loop [1]	
	e.g.	
7 b	Appropriate use of a sequence. [1]	5
	Appropriate use of selection:	
	Appropriate condition [1]	
	If true [1]	
	If false [1]	
	Loop [1]	

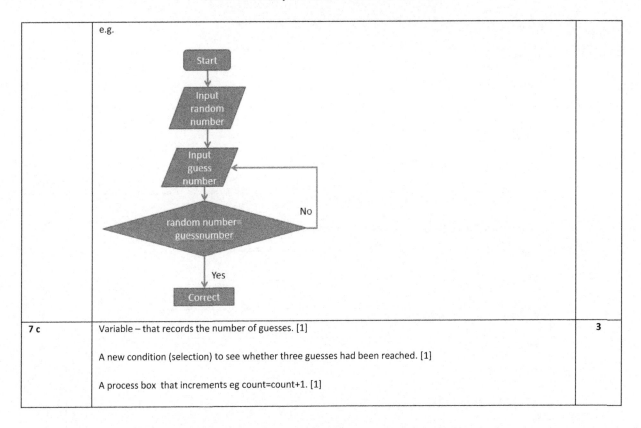

| 7 c | Variable – that records the number of guesses. [1]

 A new condition (selection) to see whether three guesses had been reached. [1]

 A process box that increments eg count=count+1. [1] | 3 |

Question Number	2.2 Programming Techniques - **Mark Scheme**	Mark
1 a	**Variable** - Variables are used to store a value. The value can change as the program is executed. [1] **Identifier**- An identifier is the label/name/text given to a variable, function, array etc. [1] **Assignment**- A value can be assigned to a variable. [1] **Constant**- The value stored cannot be altered by the program during normal execution – the value is constant. [1]	4
1 b	i-rad, area [2] ii-pi [1] iii-3.14 [1] iv-rad [1] v-area [1]	6
2 a	A Iteration. [1] B Sequence. [1]	3

	C Selection. [1]	
2 b	Iteration – Line 2. [1] Selection – Line 4. [1]	2
3	12 [1] Ada [1]	2
4 a	The program makes x the first line of text.txt. [1]	1
4 b	The program will print out the contents of text.txt. [1]	1
4 c	In the program Canada Water is made the contents of text.txt (any previous contents are overwritten). [1]	1
5 a	10 records [1] 7 Fields [1]	1
5 b	Any appropriate [1]	1
5 c	One from - String, text, alpha-numeric	1
6 a	CREATE TABLE Personal_Info (ID int(4), First_name varchar(20), [1] Surname varchar(20), [1] Age int(3), [1] Postcode varchar (8));[1]	4
6 b	First Name / Age Joanne 14 Aisha 15 Stephanie 15 Lucy 16 First name and age field only [1] Data correct [1] Ordered by age [1]	3
6 c	First Name / Surname / Age Lucy / Grant / 16 First name, surname and age field only [1] Data correct [1]	2

6 d	The wildcard uses the * symbol [1]	3
	It is used in place of any number of unknown characters. [1]	
	e.g. the following code searches for all first names with the letter "a":	
	WHERE ((Personal_info.First Name) LIKE "*a*"); [1]	
6 e	INSERT INTO personal_info [1]	2
	VALUES (1021, "Jean", "Johnson", 14, "E9 1QY"); [1]	
6 f	UPDATE Personal_Info [1]	3
	SET Personal_info.Postcode = " E17 6WS " [1]	
	WHERE Programmes.ID = 1013; [1]	
7 a	A one-dimensional array is a series of data elements organised in a row. [1]	2
	A two-dimensional array can be visualised as a grid (or table) of data elements organised with rows and columns. [1]	
7 b	Paul is 12	2
	Phillip is 15	
	Paula is 11	
	Phillipa is 14	
	All correct [2] Three correct [1]	
7c	Radius	4
	[1, 2, 3]	
	Circumference	
	[6.3, 12.6, 18.8]	
	Area	
	[3.1, 12.6, 28.3]	
	1 mark for radius, circumference and area 3 marks for correct data	
8 a	Functions return values, unlike procedures which do not. [1]	1
8 b	When you "call" a function you are telling the program to execute that function. [1]	1
8 c	This function squares the variable number. [1]	1
9 a	Casting means the changing an entity of one data type into another. [1] E.g. conversion of an integer value into a floating point value or a string.	1

9 b	Item	Data Type		8
	Surname	str		
	Telephone number	str		
	Is the sensor detecting light?	bool		
	Number of people in a car	int		
	Value of Pi to two decimal places	float		
	Postcode	str		
	Is the circuit open or closed?	bool		
	Population of greenfly	Int		
	1 mark for each correct answer.			
10 a	Anything appropriate 1 mark for each.			6
10 b	4 0 1 2 2 9 1 mark for each			6
11 a	No [1] No [1] Yes [1]			3
11 b	No [1] Yes [1] Yes [1] Yes [1]			4

Question Number	2.3 Producing Robust Programs - Mark Scheme			Mark
1 a	Defensive design is used to ensure that a piece of software functions under any circumstances.[1] It is used where it is important that software is available all of the time and is secure. [1]			2

1 b				10
	Term	**Definition**	**Example**	
	Validation	Checks if the input meets a set of criteria	Anything suitable	
	Sanitization	Modifies the input to ensure that it is valid	Anything suitable	
	Planning for contingencies	Preparing for a possible future issue with hardware or software.	Anything suitable	
	Anticipating misuse	Ensuring that the computer system is prepared for the misuse of the system by external sources.	Anything suitable	
	Authentication	Ensuring that the system is only accessible to users who pass a security test.	Anything Sensible	

2 a	Comments [1] Indentation [1] Formatting [1] Max 2			2

3 a	Testing is required to make sure that that a program functions correctly. [1] Meets the needs of the end user. [1] Max 1			1

3 b				2
	Types of testing	**Explanation**		
	Iterative Testing [1]	Testing is ongoing throughout the development process. You may code an aspect of your program and test it before moving on.		
	Final/Terminal Testing [1]	This is carried out at the end of the development process, when the program is complete, the program should be tested again (as a whole) against the requirements of the user to ensure their needs have been met.		

4 a	A **syntax** error is simply an error where the code written doesn't meet the rules of the **programming** language. These errors appear when the source code is **translated** into machine code. The translator tries to **convert** the			6

	code, but if the code doesn't meet the rules of the translator, it throws up an error. A **logic** error is one where the code is written in accordance with the programming rules and is therefore translated and runs, however, the program produces **unexpected** results.	
| 4b | ```
import turtle
def sq():
    for n in range(4):
        turtle.forward(100)
        turtle.right(90)
sq()
``` | 2 |
| 4 c | ```
def ask(q,c):
    answer=input(q)
    if answer==c:
        print("Correct!")
ask("What is 2+2?","4")
``` | 3 |
5 a	Datatype is **str** and should be **int**	1
5 b	Should be (x+y)/2	1
6 a	<table><tr><th>Type of test data</th><th>Description</th><th>Example</th></tr><tr><td>Valid Data</td><td>The data should produce the expected result.</td><td>Anything suitable</td></tr><tr><td>Invalid Data</td><td>The data should produce an error.</td><td>Anything suitable</td></tr><tr><td>Borderline Data</td><td>It is important to test that data on the edge between valid and invalid are dealt with correctly by the program.</td><td>Anything suitable</td></tr></table>	6
6 b	Test number [1] Test data [1] The reason for the test [1] The expected outcome of the test [1] The actual result of the test [1] Changes required to the program [1] Max 4	4

Question Number	2.4 Computational Logic - Mark Scheme	Mark
1 a	Binary is the base 2 number system – it consists of the two numbers 1 and 0 [1]	2
1 b	Binary numbers are required for computer logic to work as the number 1 can be represented as a high-voltage signal and the 0 can be represented as a low voltage signal. [1]	2

	Patterns of high and low voltage produce binary code [1]	
2 a	Output 0 [1] 1 [1]	**2**
2 b	Output 0 [1] 0 [1] 0 [1] 1 [1]	**4**
2 c	Output 0 [1] 1 [1] 1 [1] 1 [1]	**4**
3 a	(i) 8 [1] (ii) 22 [1] (iii) but NOT [1] (iv) 45 [1]	**4**
3 b	(i) false [1] (ii) true[1] (iii) true [1]	**3**

4 a

Door opened	Window opened	Alarm sounds		**4**
T	T	T [1]		
T	F	T [1]		
F	T	T [1]		
F	F	F [1]		

4 b				4

X	Y	NOT(X OR Y)
T	T	F [1]
F	T	F [1]
T	F	F [1]
F	F	T [1]

5 a		2

Correct use of NOT gates [1]

Correct use of AND gate [1]

5 b i		3

Correct use of NOT gate for A. [1]

No NOT gate for B. [1]

OR gate in correct location. [1]

5 b ii			4

Input		Output
A	B	Q
0	0	1 [1]
0	1	1 [1]
1	0	0 [1]
1	1	1 [1]

6 a	The DIV operator is used for finding the "quotient" [1] The MOD operator is used for finding "remainder" [1]	2

| 6 b | (i) 182 [2]

(ii) 2200 [2]

(iii) 86 [2]

(iv) 2 [2] | 8 |

Question Number	2.5 Translators and facilities of languages - **Mark Scheme**	Mark
1 a	input data [1] output data [1] process calculations [1] process decisions based on certain conditions being met [1] process repetition [1] Max 3 marks	3
1 b	<table><tr><th>High-Level</th><th>Low-Level</th></tr><tr><td>Easier to learn Similar to human language Slow to execute Easy to change To write a program you do not need knowledge of hardware Used to write applications</td><td>Difficult to learn Not similar to human language Fast to execute Difficult to change Programs include link to hardware Used to write hardware programs</td></tr></table>	6
1 c	Java, JavaScript, C++, Ruby, BASIC, Python etc 1 mark for each Max 3	3
2	They convert/translate high-level code [1] into machine code [1] They maintain the function/logic of the original code. [1]	3
3 a	Assembly language is a low-level language that relates to the operation of the CPU. [1] An assembler translates assembly language [1] into machine code (a pattern of bits that the computer's processor can use to perform its basic operations).[1]	1
3 b	An assembler translates assembly language [1] into machine code (a pattern of bits that the computer's processor can use to perform its basic operations).[1]	2

4		Compiler	Interpreter	10
	Function	A compiler translates the whole program into machine code before the program is run.	An interpreter translates code into machine code, instruction by instruction - the CPU executes each instruction before the interpreter moves on to translate the next instruction.	
	Error checking	Difficult to test individual lines of compiled code as all bugs are reported after the program has been compiled.	Interpreted code will show an error as soon as it hits a problem, so it is easier to debug than compiled code.	
	Speed	Compilation is slow but machine code can be executed quickly.	Interpreted code is slower to execute than compiled code.	
	Examples	Java and C++	JavaScript, PHP, Python and Ruby.	
	Use	Used where high speed and performance are crucial	Used for dynamic web applications.	

5 a	An integrated development environment (IDE) is an application used to create and develop software. [1]	1
5 b i	The IDE has a text edit area [1] that allows developers to write, edit and save a document of code. [1]	2

5 b ii	Feature	Explanation	3
	Auto-completion	As you start to type the first part of say a procedure, it suggests or completes the procedure.	
	Bracket matching	If you forget to close a bracket while writing, coloured highlighting may help you to detect missing brackets.	
	Syntax checks	This recognises incorrect use of syntax and highlights any errors.	

5 c	A runtime environment allows you to execute the program one step at a time. [1] This is useful to test that the code is working line by line before creating the final complete program.[1]	2

Question Number	2.6 Data representation - Mark Scheme	Mark
1 a	All in the correct order [2] One error [1]	2
1 b i	1024 [1]	1

1 b ii	8192 [1]	1
1 c i	8 x 1024 =8192 Bytes Bits=8192x8=65,536 [2]	2
1 c ii	290x1024=296,960 Bytes Bits=296,960x8=2,375,680 [2]	2
1 c iii	3x1024=3,072 Kilobytes 3,072x1024=3,145,728 Bytes 3,145,728x8=25,165,824 Bits [2]	2
2	Computers use electrical signals that are on (1) or off (0) [1] Computers therefore can only interpret binary numbers. [1]	2
3 a i	00001010 [1]	1
3 a ii	00011011 [1]	1
3 a iii	01100100 [1]	1
3 a iv	11101000 [1]	1
3 b i	42 [1]	1
3 b ii	8 [1]	1
3 b iii	147 [1]	1
3 b iv	188 [1]	1
4 a i	00010010 [1]	1
4 a ii	01111100 [1]	1
4 a iii	00011010 [1]	1
4 a iv	100111101 [1]	1
4 b	Overflow errors occur when the largest number that a register can hold is exceeded. [1] Suitable example [1]	2
5 a i	6F [2]	2

5 a ii	6C [2]	2
5 a iii	81 [2]	2
5 a iv	F4 [2]	2
5 b i	138 [2]	2
5 b ii	98 [2]	2
5 b iii	241 [2]	2
5 b iv	154 [2]	2
6 a i	55 [2]	2
6 a ii	8F [2]	2
6 a iii	1E [2]	2
6 a iv	FE [2]	2
6 b i	0110 1011 [2]	2
6 b ii	1000 1001 [2]	2
6 b iii	1011 1011 [2]	2
6 b iv	0001 1101 [2]	2
7	This is used when you want to be sure that a range of numbers has been entered correctly. [1] e.g. ISBN numbering system for books makes use of 'Modulo-11' division. if the remainder returned is incorrect the number entered is incorrect [1]	2
8 a	ASCII (American Standard Code for Information Interchange) is the most common format for defining characters in computer text files. [1] Each alphabetic, numeric, or special character is represented with a 7 bit binary number (8 bit for extended ASCII) [1]	2
8 b	Extended ASCII can code double the number of characters (256) as standard ASCII (128). [1]	1

8 c	This is an international encoding standard for use with different languages [1] by which each character is assigned a unique binary value. [1]	3
	It can code for 120,000 characters and therefore can store character coding for all languages. [1]	
9 a	Pixels are the building blocks of digital images. [1]	1
9 b	2 [1]	1
9 c	16 [1]	1
9 d	1,073,741,823 (1.073 billion colours)	1
10 a	Camera type, GPS co-ordinates, data, time, exposure, Shutter speed	4
11 a	Data is transmitted across the internet as **bits** (0s and 1s) and the **speed** is measured as bits per second. The more bits that are **transmitted** per second the faster the internet connection. How long it takes to send a file to a mobile phone over a 4G network is determined by the bandwidth. Bandwidth is a measure of how quickly **data** can be downloaded or **uploaded**. It is usually measured as bits per second (bps) or megabits per second (mbps). File sizes are measured in **bytes** (B) rather than bits (b).	6
11 b i	Microphone [1]	1
11 b ii	Digital signal [1]	1
11 b iii	The bit rate of a file tells us how many bits of data are processed every second. [1]	1
11 b iv	The number of audio samples captured every second [1]	1
11 b v	The quality of the sound recording deteriorates. [1]	1
12 a	Compression is needed for reducing file sizes. When images, sounds or videos are compressed, data is removed to reduce the file size. [1]	1
12 b	Videos are compressed when they are streamed. [1]	2
	Streaming video requires a high-speed internet connection. Without it, the user would experience buffering and regular drops in quality.[1]	
12 c	Lossless - the audio quality remains the same - it does not get worse. [1] The file can be restored back to its original state [1] Lossy - Permanently removes data. [1] The file cannot be restored. [1]	2

Printed in Great Britain
by Amazon